AF271195

Terrance Talks Travel: The Quirky Tourist Guide to Cape Town

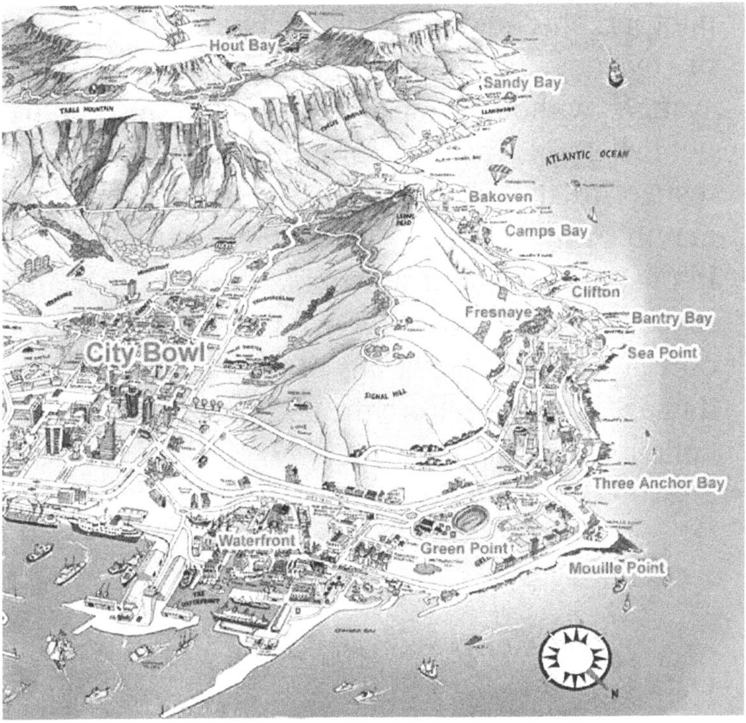

Terrance Zepke

Copyright © 2018 by Terrance Zepke

All queries should be directed to: www.safaripublishing.net.

Library of Congress Cataloging-in-Publication Data

Zepke, Terrance
Terrance Talks Travel: The Quirky Tourist Guide to Cape Town

ISBN: 978-1-942738-44-2

1. Travel-South Africa. 2. Adventure Travel. 3. Cape Town. 4. Cape Town Beaches. 5. Republic of South Africa. 6. Cape Town Wildlife. 7. Cape Town Guidebook. 9. Safari-Africa. 10. Cape Town Attractions. 11. Cape Winelands. I. Title.

First edition

Safari Publishing

CONTENTS

INTRODUCTION

This book was written with the quirky tourist in mind rather than the average tourist. *What is a quirky tourist?* A quirky tourist is anyone who likes to see and do zany, bizarre, different, fun, unique, strange, weird, and/or unusual things.

In this reference, I have included all the usual touristy stuff because most of us want to do those things. But some of us are searching for more. You know who you are. You are willing to go miles out of your way to see weird stuff that most folks don't even know about. You scour the Internet before every trip searching for anything out of the ordinary. You seek out local delicacies that others may go out of their way to avoid, such as Koesisters and Bobotie. You search for a restaurant or after hours spot that has an irresistible gimmick. You embrace new experiences. You have your limits but are game for anything that is not too physically challenging or wild and crazy. Quirky locals are

5

drawn to you, which is good because there's nothing you love more than meeting colorful characters. You dare to trod off the beaten path and see what happens.

Good for you! That's what travel is all about. And that's what this book is all about. I reveal the best of Cape Town, which is a lot. Cape Town is one the best cities in the world. It offers something for everyone, from underground tunnel tours to abseiling off Table Mountain. There are many unique restaurants (I'll tell you about a place that offers a fourteen-course tourist menu so you can sample all kinds of yummy African cuisine) and a huge variety of lodging options, from hostels to mansions. You can even stay in a pod room! I will reveal the best dance club, the best place to have brunch, best coffee bar, best adventure tour, best bookstore, and much more.

If you are planning to visit other parts of the South Africa, you may want to get my book, *TERRANCE TALKS TRAVEL: A Pocket Guide to South Africa.* It discusses everything of interest in the Republic of South Africa, including Cape Town. This reference expands on that discussion and focuses on quirky tourism. It can be a companion guide or a stand-alone reference for those traveling exclusively to Cape Town or perhaps visiting Cape Town and participating in a safari. As a bonus, I have included a "Safari Sampler" at the back of this reference. No trip to Africa is complete without participating in a safari, at least in my opinion. I have traveled the world and enjoyed many incredible adventures, but none as much as an African safari. FYI: There are many types of safaris.

So read on to learn how to make the most out of your time in Cape Town and learn more about safaris. Pay special attention to my TOP TEN PICKS, Annual Events, and FYI boxes.

GETTING THERE

It's a long way from everywhere! Visiting Cape Town is as much about the journey as the destination. This is because it is literally at the southernmost tip of South Africa. When the highway ends, you know you have arrived.

Distance from Cape Town to...
Stellenbosch (Cape Winelands)=25 miles
Port Elizabeth=412 miles
Johannesburg=785 miles
Durban=790 miles
Dar es Salaam (Tanzania)=2,293 miles
Nairobi (Kenya)=2,542 miles
Delhi (India)=5,770
London (England)=5,988 miles
Sydney (Australia)=6,856 miles
New York City (USA)=7,800

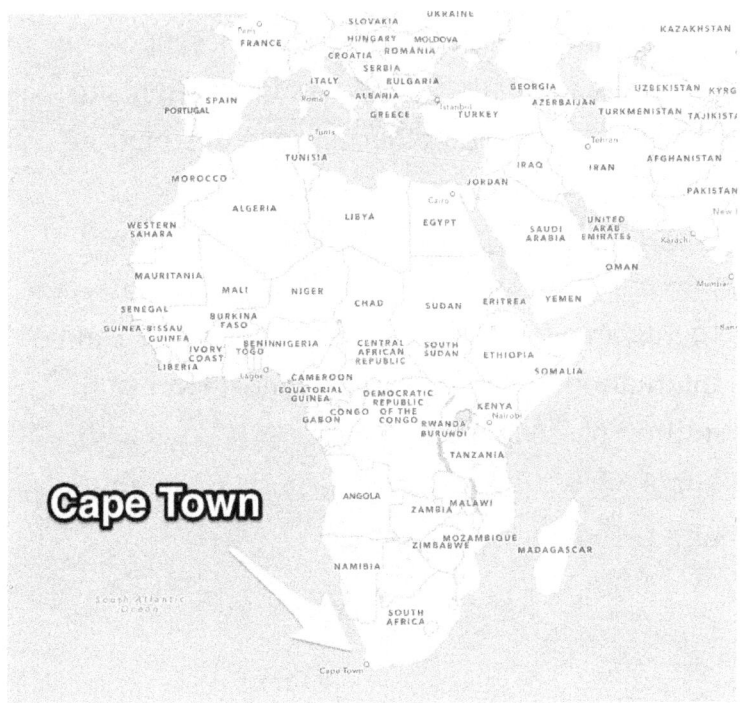

By Air

The Cape Town International Airport is on Douglas Boulevard, twelve miles from the city center. It is the second busiest airport in South Africa (Johannesburg is #1) and the third busiest in Africa. The route between Cape Town and

Johannesburg is the ninth busiest air route in the world. An estimated 4.5 million passengers fly this route annually. There are direct flights to Durban and several other African destinations, as well as to Asia and Europe. http://www.airports.co.za/airports/cape-town-international. However, most international flights arrive in Johannesburg. The O.R. Tambo International Airport serves almost twenty million passengers per year. http://www.airports.co.za/airports/or-tambo-international.

By Land

If you're planning on driving to Cape Town, I suggest you use Drive South Africa, https://www.drivesouthafrica.co.za/driving-information/street-map-directions-south-africa/, to get precise directions from your starting point to your final destination in or around Cape

Town. This site even tells you how much money you'll spend on tolls and fuel.

FYI: Be advised that it is approximately a fourteen-hour drive from Johannesburg to Cape Town. Beaufort West and Hanover are good stopovers on this route and Addo National Park or Golden Gate Highlands National Park are good safari stops.

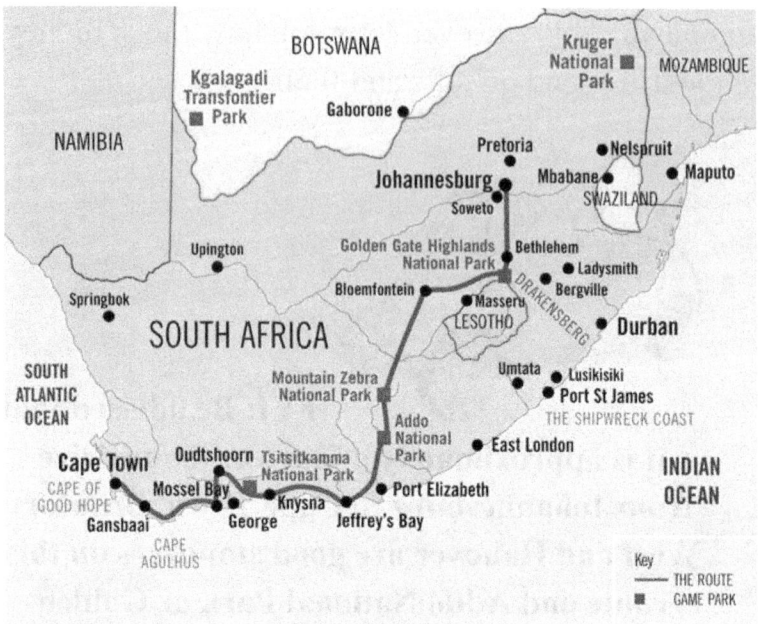

This map shows you the best route if you are driving from Johannesburg and planning on going to any safari parks (game drives) on route to Cape Town.

<u>More Options</u>

There are some great train trips: Rovos Rail, https://www.rovos.com/journeys/cape-town, and the **Blue Train,** http://www.bluetrain.co.za/, and **Shosholoza Meyl Railways**, https://www.shosholozameyl.co.za/train-routes.html. **Shongololo Express**, www.shongololo.com.

GETTING AROUND

Once in Cape Town, the best way to get around is on foot or the city bus. There is a rail system, but it is unreliable. http://myciti.org.za/en/home/

TERRANCE'S TOP TEN PICKS

1. **Take a Cape Peninsula Tour**. One of my favorite experiences is driving Chapman's Peak to Cape Point. During this twenty-five mile scenic drive, you'll pass Millionaires Paradise (a stretch of coast filled with expensive homes from Clifton to Camps Bay). This is *literally* a breath-

taking view as there are no guard rails along the cliffs. During this drive, you'll see Green Point and Sea Point, Hout Bay, Noordhoek, Simon's Town (including Boulder's Beach and African Penguins), Fish Hoek Beach, and Muizenberg. Be sure to stop and take a seal island cruise. There is wildlife at Cape Point, such as ostriches, Cape Mountain Zebras, and baboons. Be sure to allow enough time as there is much to see and do at Cape Point. In fact, several of my TOP TEN PICKS involve Cape Point.

2. At Cape Point, ride the cable car, *Flying Dutchman* (named after a legendary ghost ship), up to the top where there is a historic old lighthouse and the best view of the

Cape. Even if you decide to hike, you should ride the cable car one-way.

3. At Cape Point, dine and shop from the top. Have lunch or dinner at Two Oceans Restaurant, and you will enjoy a panoramic view and delicious food. Shop for souvenirs and novelty gifts at the large gift shop at the top of the cliff. The selection is great, and the price is even better. If there is bad weather or you don't have time to go to the top, there are two shops at the base of the mountain.

4. At Cape Point, pose for a picture in front of the Latitude and Longitude sign for Cape of Good Hope.

5. Look for flora and fauna, wildlife and shipwrecks. There are 250 bird species here, as well as ostriches, baboons, elands

(largest mammal in the world), and the Cape Mountain Zebra. Beware of the baboons! They can be mean if you get too close and steal your stuff. You'll also find more than 1,000 indigenous plants that don't grow anywhere else in the world. If you take shipwreck trail, you will have a chance to view some of the recorded shipwrecks around Cape Point.

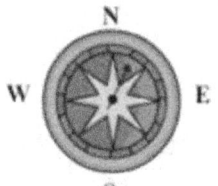 **FYI: The southernmost tip of Africa is not Cape of Good Hope! It lies 155 kilometers southeast of Cape Point at Cape Agulhas.**

When this was realized, the government barely acknowledged this distinction except to change the sign at Cape of Good Hope to read *"The Most South-Western Point of The African Continent."*

* * *

6. **Robben Island** is seven miles from Cape Town in the middle of Table Bay. The tours are led by former political prisoners, so you will get the real story about the island prison. Tours include the leprosy graveyard, Lime Quarry, army and navy bunkers, Bluestone Quarry, and the

maximum security prison that includes
Nelson Mandela's cell.

See listing under 'Touristy Things to Do'
for more information. http://robben-island.org.za/tours

**Robben Island with Table Mountain in
background**

7. Take an **underground tour of Cape Town** that extends from Buitkenkant Street all the way to the Castle of Good Hope. In addition to these tunnel tours, Good Hope Adventures also offers bicycle, snorkeling, and tobogganing tours. Thrill seekers will delight in their wind-powered beach buggy and sandboarding adventures. Sandboarding is similar to snowboarding only on sand rather than snow. http://goodhopeadventures.com/tunnel-tours

**FYI: A cannon is fired every day at
noon from Signal Hill. This is an old
Capetonian tradition. Just before noon,
an officer from Lion's Battery loads a
little powder bag into the cannon
barrel. The cannon automatically
ignites and fires at 12:00 P.M. sharp
when the Cape Town Observatory
sends an electronic signal to the gun.**

8. Explore **Kirstenbosch National
   Botanical Garden,** including its
   Centenary Tree Canopy Walkway. This
   walkway takes visitors from the forest
   floor up into the trees where Garden and
   Cape Flats can be seen from the canopy.
   This elevated walkway thrills visitors
   because it winds and dips like a snake.

More than just a garden, Kirstenbosch is part of a nature reserve and one of the greatest botanical gardens in the world. More than 7,000 rare and threatened species can be found here. Established in 1913, it is the first botanical garden to be listed as a UNESCO World Heritage Site. There are several good shops and restaurants at Kirstenbosch. It's an amazing place.

http://www.sanbi.org/gardens/kirstenbosch

**King Protea is a gorgeous plant that is indigenous to
South Africa.**

9. Enjoy **high tea** in grand style. The best places for afternoon tea are Mount Nelson Hotel, Table Bay Hotel, and Cape Grace Hotel. Mount Nelson Hotel on Orange Street has a signature tea blended from six black teas (Darjeeling, Kenya, Assam, Keemun, Yunnan, and Ceylon), plus rose petals from their garden. Cape Grace Hotel (best homemade scones) and Table Bay Hotel (three courses including a huge buffet table of sweets) are on the V & A Waterfront. Even if you're not a tea connoisseur, you should go because it is a lovely afternoon treat. Wine and champagne can be added to afternoon tea for a reasonable rate. These are among the finest hotels in Cape Town so be prepared to be impressed. If tea is just not your

thing, how about tasting some of Cape
Town's renowned cuisine? See Touristy
Things to Do for a list of possibilities,
including the **Cape Town Foodie Tasting
Tour**.

FYI: Rooibos tea or red tea is a medicinal, herbal beverage that is acquired from the Aspalathus linearis bush plant that is found in South Africa. According to the South African Rooibos Council, rooibos is not a true tea, but a herb. Don't tell Afrikaans that because they call it tea! But it is true that Rooibos tea has lots of health benefits.

10. From high tea to high mountain—**go abseiling down Table Mountain**. One of the top attractions in the Cape Town area is Table Mountain. Most folks take the cable car up or hike one of the trails to the top, but daring souls go abseiling. As you descend, you will not be afraid, but amazed by the dazzling view. You will see Cape Town, Camps Bay, and the Atlantic Seaboard. It is a thrilling experience, and you do not need to have any previous abseiling experience. Participants are trained and briefed beforehand as to what to expect.

http://www.abseilafrica.co.za/

Table Mountain

FYI: Table Mountain is older than the Andes,
the Alps, the Rocky Mountains and the
Himalayas. We're talking more than 260
million years old. At least one wedding per
week takes place on the summit. It is the only
mountain to be included in the list of seven
natural wonders, and one of the few
mountains to be situated within a major city.

TOURISTY THINGS TO SEE & DO

Adderley Street is also easy to identify as it is the flower market, so visitors can see and smell gorgeous flowers of every imaginable kind. It is considered the main street of Cape Town.

Bo-Kaap is an area of Cape Town formerly known as the Malay Quarter. It is a former township, situated on the slopes of Signal Hill above the city center and is a historical center of Cape Malay culture in Cape Town. It is known for its colorful townhouses. The Bo-Kaap Museum, which features exhibits about Malay history, is on Wales Street.

FYI: Hipsters will want to go to the bohemian suburbs of Woodstock and Observatory because they are full of art galleries, fashion studios, and trendy bars and cafés.

Castle of Good Hope is the oldest edifice in South Africa. This castle fortress, built in the late 1600s, is now a museum and popular tourist attraction. http://www.castleofgoodhope.co.za/

Castle of Good Hope

FYI: If you buy a "hop on, hop off" bus pass, it includes stops at all the major tourist attractions, which are too spread out to explore by foot. The pass allows visitors to "hop on and hop off as they please. Tourists can purchase a one-day pass or a multi-day pass.

Additionally, passengers are given headphones so they can enjoy an audio tour of Cape Town, which discusses the history and important facts about each place. However, both the Blue Bus and the Red Bus (two different routes) only go in one direction, so be prepared to ride the entire route or walk back to your destination. You can also opt for a harbor cruise. http://www.city-sightseeing.com/tours/south-africa/cape-town.htm

City Hall overlooks the Grand Parade. It was built in 1905, and the bell tower was added in 1923. The Italian Renaissance structure faces four different streets.

District Six Museum serves to commemorate the former District Six are of Cape Town. At one time, it was home to more than ten percent of the city's population. The museum was established in 1994 when apartheid finally ended. It has an incredible collection of street signs, photographs, documents, and recordings. http://www.districtsix.co.za/

Grand Parade is the main public square in Cape Town and also the oldest. The square is surrounded by Cape Town City Hall, the Castle of Good Hope, and the Cape Town Railway Station. Markets are held in the square a couple of times a week. Vendors sell flowers, food, handicrafts, and more. The square is also used for political rallies. Nelson Mandela held his first public address here after being released from prison in 1990. It was once a fort and exercise area for troops.

The tower of The Cape Town City Hall has a marble façade and turret clock with a face created from skeleton iron dials filled with opal. The building was constructed from limestone imported from England. It houses the library and concert hall.

Greenmarket Square is a large open-air craft market featuring African curios, leather goods, clothes, paintings, and other artwork.

House of Parliament is the official seat of the South African government. This building dates back to 1884.

Iziko Slave Lodge was once slave quarters for those working in the Company's Garden. Today, Company's Garden is a large public park that includes botanical gardens. Don't be surprised if squirrels approach you (standing on their hind legs) to beg for a treat. Warning! I have seen squirrls jump in the laps of people who are sitting on a bench eating any kind of food. *Seriously!*

Iziko South African Museum and Planetarium has a bit of everything about natural history, from rock art to reptile fossils. http://www.iziko.org.za/

Iziko South African National Gallery features temporary and permanent collections of British, French, Dutch, Flemish, and South African paintings, sculptures, textiles, photography, beadwork, and more.

http://www.iziko.org.za/museums/south-african-national-gallery

Kirstenbosch National Botanical Garden is situated at the base of Table Mountain. This 1,300-acre garden dates back to 1913, and since that time it has only cultivated indigenous plants. It is the most famous national botanical garden in South Africa and also contains a conservatory. http://www.sanbi.org/gardens/kirstenbosch

Long Street is one of the main streets of the city and can be easily recognized even without a map as the street is lined with exquisite Victorian buildings, which include intricate wrought-iron balconies and other special features. At one time, it was the longest street in the city.

Robben Island is seven miles from Cape Town in the middle of Table Bay. The tours are led by former political prisoners, so you will learn a lot. Tours begin at the Nelson Mandela Gateway at the V & A Waterfront. Participants get off the

ferry and board buses at Murray's Bay Harbour,
which is on the east side of the island. The bus
tour approximately three hours and include the
leprosy graveyard (the island was a leper colony
at one time), Lime Quarry, army and navy
bunkers, Bluestone Quarry, lighthouse,
Governor's House, and maximum security
prison, including Nelson Mandela's cell..
http://robben-island.org.za/tours

**Robben Island is where Nelson Mandela spent part of
his 27-year prison term.**

South African Jewish Museum offers interactive exhibits chronicling the history of Jews in South Africa. http://www.sajewishmuseum.org.za/

St. George's Mall can also be easily recognized as it is home to many street performers and has a huge pedestrian area in its center.

Table Mountain overlooks Cape Town and is part of Table Mountain National Park. Its most noticeable feature is its level plateau that extends two miles and is flanked to the east by Devil's Peak and to the west by Lion's Head (more about Table Mountain later in this chapter). https://www.sanparks.org/parks/table_mountain/tourism/attractions.php

Two Oceans Aquarium is on the V & A Waterfront. The southern tip of the African continent is the meeting place of two mighty and bountiful oceans, the Indian and the Atlantic. This aquarium shows the incredible diversity of marine life found in these two oceans. See penguins, sharks, and more. www.aquarium.co.za

V & A Waterfront is home to Table Bay Hotel, Victoria Wharf Shopping Centre, Amphitheatre, Cape Grace Hotel, Cape Town Diamond Museum and that is Table Mountain in the background.

Two Oceans Aquarium. As the name implies, the aquarium has aquatic displays from both the

Indian and Atlantic Oceans, including penguins and sharks.

Many different religions are practiced in Cape Town, so lots of different religious structures can be found, such as **The Mosque in Longmarket Street**, **Lutheran Church** on Strand Street, and **St. George's Cathedral**, which is an Anglican cathedral with beautiful stained glass. **Groote Kerk** is South Africa's oldest church. Only the steeple remains from the original church, which was rebuilt circa 1840. Regardless of your religious beliefs, you should appreciate the architectural beauty of many of these buildings.

FYI: There is a large gay population in Cape Town. The visitor's center offers Pink Maps that highlight places of particular interest to gay visitors, such as an area of town known as De Waterkant.

Blue Crane is the National Bird of South Africa

* * *

Warning: *Make sure that Table Mountain is open before setting out. The mountain often closes due to high winds, even if it isn't windy in town. Conditions change fast and fog often appears, blanketing the mountain and earning it the nickname 'Table Cloth.' The cable car does not operate in bad weather.*

There are a hundred different paths to the top of Table Mountain, but the most popular ones are clearly denoted. It takes an average of three hours to ascend to the top. You can even do both if you like. You can take the cable car up the mountain and then meander down the mountain on foot or hike up to the top and take the cable car down. If it is a nice day, be sure to do Table Mountain even if you had planned to see other sights as the weather is unpredictable in Cape Town. There are posted signs that will let you know if the mountain is closed.
www.sanparks.org/parks/table_mountain

More You Should Know About Table Mountain

Table Mountain National Park runs north-south along the Cape Peninsula. The park is separated by urban areas so it is made up of three different areas:

1. Table Mountain (including Signal Hill, Lion's Head, and Table Mountain)
2. Silvermine-Tokai (Silvermine Nature Reserve is part of Table Mountain)
3. Cape Point (Cape Peninsula)

FYI: A popular activity for those in good shape is to hike Lion's Head by moonlight.

There are lots of activities you can do in and around Cape Town, such as a sunset picnic at Camps Bay, horseback riding on Noordhoek Beach, surfing at Big Bay, shark cage diving, watching the African penguins at Boulder's Beach, and sandboarding at Betty's Bay. For a list of resources visit www.capetown.travel. For a list of extreme sports, such as kloofing and skydiving, check out http://www.uncoverthecape.co.za/extreme.htm.

There is an old legend about a Dutchman named Jan van Hunks, who got into a smoking contest with a stranger while up at Devil's Peak. The competition went on for days before the stranger admitted defeat and confessed his identity. He introduced himself as the Devil just before scooping up the Dutchman and disappearing into a cloud of smoke. Bellowing puffs of smoke lingered there long after they were gone. According to legend, when Devil's Peak is blanketed in clouds, it is believed to be the Devil coming back.

Cape Town is in South Africa's Western Cape. The following places are also in the Western Cape and close to Cape Town. They are on the Garden Route, which refers to the coastline that meanders from Mossel Bay (just outside Cape Town) to Grahamstown. Tourists appreciate the scenic 150-mile drive because the route is between the ocean and the mountains, so there is plenty to see and do along the way. www.gardentroute.org. Here are the highlights:

Addo Elephant National Park is one of the biggest tourist attractions in this region and home to one of the largest elephant populations in South Africa. www.addoelephantpark.com

Cango Caves are near the town of Oudtshoorn, in the Western Cape Province of South Africa. Visitors are only permitted to go in supervised groups. There is a Standard Tour and an Adventure Tour. The adventure tour includes some crawling through narrow passageways and climbing steep rock formations guided only by small lights.

Cape Columbine Lighthouse, commissioned on October 1, 1936, is the last manned beacon in South Africa. It also holds the distinction of being

the first lighthouse to receive three navigational
aids: a fog signal, radio beacon, and light.

Many believe that no visit to South Africa is
complete without a trip through the **Cape
Winelands**. There are plenty of places to visit
given that there are five dozen wineries in
Stellenbosch, two dozen wineries in
Franschhoek, and seventeen in Paarl. The climate
and soil of the Western Cape make this region one
of the best wine-producing places in the world. It
is ideal for growing Sauvignon Blanc,
Chardonnay, Cabernet Sauvignon, Shiraz and
Pinot Noir. A large number of the vineyards have
restaurants on site. Some offer cheese tastings in
addition to wine tastings. Typically, there is a
small fee charged but may be refunded if wine is
purchased or the fee is included if taking a Cape
Winelands tour. The Cape Winelands are easily
accessible from Cape Town and can be explored
independently or on a tour. Most of the vineyards
are open during the week and some on weekends.

You can even hot-air balloon over the Cape Winelands. www.wineland.co.za

Grahamstown has more than fifty churches and sixty national monuments.

Knysna Forest is considered the 'pearl' of the Garden Route. Located between George and Plettenberg Bay, it is known for its ancient yellowwood trees and stinkwood trees. The forest is home to more than 230 species of birds.

Oudtshoorn is the largest town in the Little Karoo region; home to approximately 60,000 residents. Its largest non-human population is the ostrich since this is where most breeding farms in South Africa can be found. There are more than four hundred ostrich farms here with the biggest being Highgate Ostrich Show Farm and Safari Show Farm. www.outdtshoorn.info

FYI: If you visit an ostrich farm at Oudtshoorn, be warned that ostriches eat just about anything and have been known to eat sunglasses, hats, and even buttons off their jackets or shirts.

Port Elizabeth is the second largest city in this country, as far as size. Located on the Southeast coast of Africa, Port Elizabeth is a major seaport on Algoa Bay, which is the reason for its nickname "The Bay." It was established in 1820 to house British settlers. It is now part of the Nelson Mandela Bay Metropolitan Municipality, which has well over one million residents. It is best known for the many watersports it offers, as well as Shamwari Game Reserve, where the 'Big

Five' can be found, as well as lots of other species of animals. www.portelizabeth.co

West Coast National Park is more than one hundred square miles. It is considered an Important Bird Area (including African Oystercatchers and African Penguins) and home to large antelope, such as Mountain Zebra, Kudu, and Red Hartebeest, as well as Cape Gray Mongoose, Flamingos, and the Caracal. www.sanparks.org

BEST OF CAPE TOWN

BEST PLACE TO SEE SHARKS: There are
several good places in South Africa to see sharks,
but Cape Town's **Gansbaai** is probably the best.
Approximately 100 miles off the coast of Cape
Town lies Dyer Island, which is home to the
largest seal colony in South Africa. Great White
Sharks can be found wherever there is food (and
they love seal meat), so sharks are abundant in
these waters. There are at least a half-dozen
companies that offer shark cage diving at 'Shark
Alley.' A couple of companies I recommend are
Shark & Safari Tours & Shuttles,
www.sharkandsafari.co.za, and Apex Shark
Expeditions, www.apexpredators.com. If you'd
like to see a shark without having to go cage-
diving, the best bet is at False Bay (Muizenberg),
where there are shark spotters on duty. Like
lifeguards, they have assigned positions along the
beach. Watch for flags on the beach, which mean
that sharks have been spotted that day. If you hear

a siren, that means a shark has just been spotted
SO GET OUT OF THE WATER
IMMEDIATELY!

**FYI: Did you know that a Great White
Shark can weigh over 7,000 pounds and be
as long as 26 feet? No wonder it is the
world's largest predatory fish!**

BEST TIME AND PLACE TO SEE WHALES:
Whale-watching is another popular pastime. Peak
whale-watching season is from mid-August to
mid-November, but it depends on the species as
to the best time because there are thirty-seven
species of dolphins and whales that can be found
in the waters around South Africa. One company
I recommend for a whale-watching cruise is New

Fusion (www.newfusion.co.za). The best place to see whales from land is from certain vantage points along Chapman's Peak Drive. Land sightings are most common at Hermanus and False Bay. Southern right and humpback whales have been seen as close as thirty feet offshore!

There is an annual Whale Festival, but there is also a Whale Crier who appears daily in Hermanus during whale watching season. He uses his special "crier" to announce whale sightings that can be seen from land.

FYI: The male reaches maturity at around 13 years old and the female at 20 years old. The average litter is 7 – 9 pups. Females reproduce only twice in their lives. Their diet consists of all other marine life! They like seals, dolphins, and all fish. They are powerful enough to be able to propel themselves all the way out of the water. They have pointed snouts and razor-sharp teeth. Roughly three dozen species of whales have been spotted around South Africa, but the most commonly seen are the humpback, southern right, orcas (killer), and Bryde's whales. The best time to see most of these is from July – November. Several species of dolphins can also be seen in these waters.

BEST PLACE TO HAVE A BEER: Brewers & Union and Power & the Glory offers craft beer, delicious hot dogs, and great music.

BEST PLACE TO HAVE A BEER IF YOU'RE A HIPSTER: Superette, Skinny Legs, and Clarkes

BEST PLACE TO HAVE A COCKTAIL:
Societi, Bistro's Snug Bar, and Rafiki's

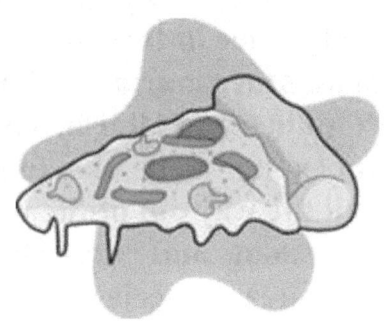

BEST PLACE FOR PIZZA: Beluga and DaVincis

BEST PLACE FOR PASTA: Cocoa Uda

BEST PLACE FOR AMBIENCE: Ritz and Greenhouse (The Cellars-Hohenorrt Hotel)

BEST BRUNCH: Skinny Legs

BEST BAKERY: Jason's Bakery (be sure to try their doughssants)

BEST PLACE FOR SALADS AND SANDWICHES: The Kitchen

BEST PLACE TO HAVE A BURGER: <u>Dog's
Bollocks</u>

BEST PLACE FOR MEXICAN: <u>El Burro </u>has
the best food and serves tequila.

BEST PLACE FOR ASIAN: <u>Tjing Torii</u> is the
place to go for sushi. Their specialty is
ochazuke, but everything is delicious in this hip
and trendy eatery.

BEST BISTRO: Mink & Trout offers simple
but divine delicacies, such as ginger-pickled
veggies with miso cream cheese; trout,
asparagus, leek-and-ricotta tart; and Karoo lamb
bredie.

**FYI: South African cuisine is a delicious fusion
of Dutch, French, British and Cape Malay
cooking borne from settlers at the Cape.**

BEST PLACE FOR COFFEE & TEA: Deluxe Coffeeworks, EspressoLab and Origin (in the back is Nigiro, a must for tea drinkers) and Lady Cupcake (for tea and best cupcakes)

BEST PLACE FOR ICE CREAM: Roxy's and Mr. Pickwicks

BEST PLACE FOR CAPE MALAY FOOD (Traditional Cape Town cuisine): Noon Gun Tea Room

FYI: Cape Malay cuisine includes rice, coconut milk, and lots of spices! Visit https://capefusiontours.com/cape-cooking-experiences/ **to find Cape Malay cooking classes and similar experiences in Cape Town.**

BEST PLACE TO SAMPLE AFRICAN CUISINE: Gold Restaurant features a fourteen-course menu showcasing foods from North Africa, Sub-Sahara Africa, and Southern Africa. Entrees include options like Tanzanian mango and lime free range chicken – fragrant with coriander and ginger – and Cape Malay seafood curry with kingklip and prawns – which is also available in a vegetarian version. http://www.goldrestaurant.co.za/.

BEST PLACE TO SHOP: There are many shops catering to tourists at Victoria & Albert Waterfront, but there is also ample shopping at Green Market Square, Long Street, Kalk Bay, and the area around Two Oceans Aquarium (and many souvenirs can be found in the aquarium's gift shop).

BEST MARKET: **Neighbourgoods Market** in the Biscuit Mill is open every Saturday. More than 100 vendors sell the finest artisan foods, ranging from meat to baked goods.

BEST PLACE FOR NIGHTLIFE: **Waiting Room, Zula Bar**, and **Dockside**, a gigantic

temple-shaped building that houses fashionable
bars, restaurants, and a huge ultra-hip discotheque
that can hold up to 5,000 people.

**BEST FOODIE TOUR: Cape Town Foodie
Tasting Walking Tour** reveals the best local
cuisine at a leisurely pace. You will also see a
lot of Cape Town and learn a lot about its food
scene. **www.capetownfoodietour.co.za**. The
best foodie tour for the Cape Winelands is **Cape
Fusion Tours.** The guided tours escort
participants from Cape Town to world renowned
wine farms. Leave the driving and logistics to
them as you sample fine wine and gourmet
cuisine. www.capefusiontours.com.

**BEST ADVENTURE TOUR: Overnight
Scenic Cederberg Explorer**. Adventure Tours
Cape Town takes participants to the picturesque
Cederberg Mountains where they'll see
imposing rock formations, centuries old rock
paintings of the Khoi-San people, and more.
Relaxing in rock pools included!

http://adventuretours.capetown/overnight-adventures/

BEST BATHHOUSE: Long Street Baths has been around since 1908. Their most popular service is a Turkish bath, but they also have steam rooms, swimming pool, and spa treatments. https://www.westerncape.gov.za/facility/long-street-baths

BEST PLACE TO SEE THE STARS: Visit the Planetarium **at Cape Town Astronomical Observatory**. A night tour is offered on the second Saturday of each month. FREE.

BEST BEACH: A tiny, but oh-so-nice beach, is **Beta Beach**. Only the locals know about this little oasis, which is perfect for having a sundowner and watching the sunset.

BEST BOOKSTORE: The **Book Lounge** is considered the best independent bookshop in all of South Africa, so it is well worth a visit. Located in an old Victorian building in Roeland Street, visitors will find every kind of book including bestsellers, coffee table books, and rare books.

BEST SPIRITUAL RETREAT: Blue Butterfly Retreat is located in the middle of Welbedacht Nature Reserve, which is about ninety minutes from Cape Town. It offers a mix of hiking, swimming, wildlife viewing, meditation, birding, biking, massage, and yoga. http://www.thebluebutterfly.co.za/index.htm

BEST PARK: Company's Garden was created by the Dutch East India Company in 1652. The gardens extend through much of Cape Town and feature monuments and exhibits, such as a Japanese flower garden, a vegetable garden, and a koi pond. It is worth going just to watch the squirrels. They will come right up to you. Literally! One sat on my lap in a beggar's pose when I sat down to eat a protein bar.

Suddenly, I was surrounded by squirrels who assumed the same beggar's pose on the ground around the bench. It was a bit creepy but mostly hilarious. These are no ordinary squirrels!

RUNNER UP: Durbanville Rose Garden is the place to go if you are into roses. There are close to 5,000 award-winning rose bushes boasting more than 500 varieties of rose. There are also hybrid tea plants and a Tea Room, which is a lovely spot to relax and enjoy the view of the park.

MILK TART (Melktert) RECIPE

(This is a yummy traditional South African dessert that is similar to a custard tart. It can be served hot or cold)

3 tablespoon butter, melted

3 egg yolks

3 egg whites

4 cups milk

1 tsp vanilla extract

1 tablespoon cinnamon sugar

1 tsp baking powder

¼ tsp salt

1 cup floor

Preheat oven to 375°. Mix butter, sugar, and yolks.
Stir in flour, baking powder, and salt. Add vanilla
and milk. In a separate bowl, whip the egg whites
until stiff. Add egg whites to batter. Pour mixture
into a nine-inch pie pan. Sprinkle cinnamon sugar
on top. Bake for 20-25 minutes and then reduce heat
to 325°. Bake another 20 minutes or until done.

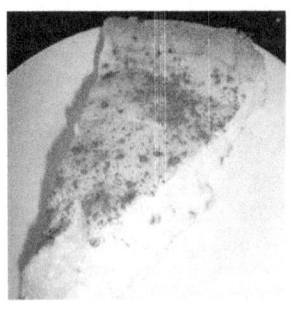

ABOUT ACCOMMODATIONS

Accommodations vary greatly in Cape Town, from self-catering apartments to deluxe five-star hotels. Tourists can choose to stay in the heart of the city or on the beach. They can stay in a small B & B or a large resort. There are so many options and a vast price range in the greater Cape Town area. The best deals are typically on vacation rentals or promotional specials found on AirBnB.com, Priceline.com, Trivago.com, Hotels.com, and Booking.com. Also, look for seasonal specials and discounted packages on resort websites. For a cosmopolitan city like Cape Town, it is surprising how many affordable lodging options there are—and it won't feel like you're skimping!

BEST HOSTEL

Once in Cape Town is so chic you won't feel like you're staying in a hostel, but your wallet will know. Its strategic location on Kloof Street makes it within walking distance of some of the best boutiques, bars, and restaurants in Cape Town. There are lots of options, such as ladies only dorms, private rooms, and family suites. Amenities include a large outdoor fire pit, a meditation garden, and kitchen. Freebies include WiFi, linen, and breakfast at their on-site café. http://onceincapetown.co.za/

BEST CAMPING/BEST VIEW

Ashanti Lodge Backpackers is situated at the base of Table Mountain in a lovely Victorian mansion with shared and private rooms. This lovely lodge has everything you need: swimming pool, garden, lounge with television, bar area, lockers, and a killer view. Plus, there are perfect places to pitch a tent if you like spending the night under the stars. http://ashanti.co.za/accommodation/backpackers-gardens/

BEST BUDGET LODGE

Never@Home Backpackers gets you the most bang for your buck. Located on Green Point strip near the V & A Waterfront, guests just have to walk outside to find lots of trendy bars, shops, and restaurants. This lodge offers shared rooms and private rooms, plus a lovely patio, complimentary toiletries, free Wi-Fi, swimming pool, kitchen, on-site bar/restaurant, and a shuttle service. http://neverathomeworld.com/

BEST ECO-FRIENDLY LODGING

Backpack & Travel is so eco-friendly that you can't beat it. They only use biodegradable cleaning products, and they recycle everything humanly possible. They even use vegetable scraps to feed their worm farms. All rooms have air conditioning and private or shared bathrooms. Amenities include free Wi-Fi, complimentary breakfast, swimming pool, billiards table, bar/café on site, kitchen, laundry facilities, luggage storage, ATM, and a travel center to assist you with the rest of your trip. https://backpackers.co.za/

BEST PLACE FOR SOCIAL BUTTERFLIES

Okay, so maybe this should be BEST PLACE TO PARTY because **Carnival Court** is known as one of the top twenty party hostels in the world. There are large balconies on both floors of this lodge that offer a lovely view of Signal Hill. Many attractions are within a five or ten-minute walk from here, but some guests choose to linger at Carnival Court and play foosball, billiards, or just meet and mingle. http://www.carnivalcourt.co.za/index.php

BEST HIPSTER HOSTEL

In the heart of Cape Town center on Long Street is **91 Loop**. It is a fairly new boutique hostel. The bus stop is right outside the front door, and there are several rooms to choose from, including ensuites and pod rooms. Guests get free breakfast daily, high-tech key-cards and lockers, 24-hour reception, airport pick-ups, free WiFi, mobile charging station, a free welcome drink and several weekly socials! South African beer and meals are served in their Honey Badger Bar and On Longmarket provides gourmet coffee without having to leave the premises. https://www.91loop.co.za/

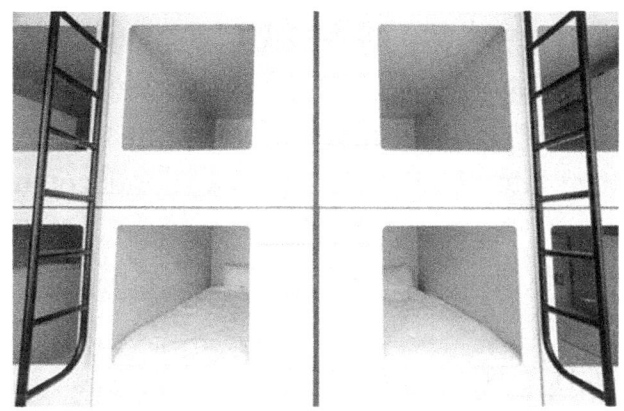

Pod rooms at 91 Loop

BEST GUESTHOUSE

Rodwell House is one of the original 1930s mansions overlooking False Bay. If you're looking for historical and charming (plus this place is loaded with too many amenities to remember), this is the place. But it is not cheap! http://www.rodwellhouse.co.za/

BEST CAMPING

Chapman's Peak Cottages & Caravan Park is an idyllic setting. Situated on a twelve-acre site surrounded by fruit and olive trees, this property is within walking distance of restaurants and within a few minutes of many Cape Town attractions. There is a playground and swimming pool on site. There are campsites and cottages, which have kitchens and TVs. http://www.capestay.co.za/chapmans-peak/

BEST B & B

Flying Penguin Simon's Town has spectacular views and is just a five-minute walk to Fisherman's Beach. It is close to Boulder's Beach and Simon's Town boutiques and cafes. Choose from standard rooms or the Penthouse. http://www.capestay.co.za/theflyingpenguin/

BEST LUXURY VILLA

Hout Mansion on Hout Bay is my pick. This place has everything. We're talking about a wine cellar, cinema, outdoor entertainment area, swimming pool, meditation space, gardens, houseman, concierge, and private chef. But it is not cheap! http://www.capestay.co.za/houtbaymansion/

BEST WATERFRONT HOTEL

This is a tough one because most of the best hotels in the city are located on the V & A Waterfront, but my pick is the **One and Only**. While it is a large hotel with plenty of amenities, it feels like you're staying in a cozy African lodge. This is thanks in large part to its décor and ambience. Some special things they offer are a wine loft, teen spa treatments, kids' programs, poolside restaurant, Vista Bar, and Nobu Restaurant, which uses South African produce in all their specialties. http://www.hotel.co.za/waterfront-accommodation-oneandonly.html

Best deals on vacation rentals can be found at:
http://vacations.capetown/
http://www.capevacationrentals.org/
www.airbnb.com/s/Cape-Town

For more lodging options visit www.capetown.travel

ABOUT CAPE TOWN

Cape Town is South Africa's oldest city, which is why it is often referred to as the "Mother City." The first Council meeting was held on a sailing ship in the middle of Cape Town's Table Bay on April 8, 1652. It was inhabited by ancestors of Kalahari Bushmen for thousands of years before being discovered by the Europeans in 1652.

A trading post was established here by the Dutch East Indies Company. It also became home to French Huguenots, who sought asylum here from religious persecution. Later, it came under British rulc. All these different influences can be seen in the architecture throughout Cape Town. Many of these historic buildings are being used as museums, monuments, and galleries. Cape Town's famous landmark, the Castle of Good Hope, is the oldest colonial building in South Africa. Construction began in 1666 and was completed in 1679. Building materials include granite, blue slate, and shells brought over from Robben Island. The fort was built by soldiers, slaves, prisoners, and volunteers. Over the years, it has served as a bakery, church, prison, shop, and other facilities. Interestingly, the Castle of Good Hope has never been attacked. It was declared a national monument in 1936.

Some of the historic structures are still being used as residences, particularly in the Bo-Kaap area, which is the oldest suburb and has a large Malay population. Ironically, the oldest street in Cape Town is Long Street, which is also considered to be the trendiest area of town.

Today, Cape Town is the second-most populated city in South Africa, just behind Johannesburg. Not only is it the legislative capital of South Africa, but it is the administrative and economic center of the Western Cape Province. Also, Cape Town is the seat of the National Parliament.

Cape Town is the number one international tourist destination in Africa. There is so much to see and do, which is why it's a favorite tourist destination. For example, the V & A Waterfront boasts more than 450 shops. There are hundreds of shops, attractions, restaurants, bars, nightclubs, and area beaches. Adventure pursuits range from shark cage diving to tobogganing (seriously!) Cape Town is consistently voted a favorite place among travelers and the media, such as *Travel and Leisure*, Trip Advisor, CNN, and *The New York Times*.

Cape Town lies on a small peninsula at the southern tip of the country. Devil's Peak is to its east while Lion's Head is to the west. Lion's Head is a mountain range that separates Camps

Bay from Sea Point. Cape Town is comprised of eight areas:

1. **Atlantic Seaboard** has been dubbed Cape Town's "Riviera." It stretches from the V & A Waterfront to the west side of Cape Peninsula, ending just before Hout Bay. It includes Green Point, Sea Point, Fresnaye, Bantry Bay, Camps Bay, Oudekraal, and Llandudno.

2. **City Centre** is commonly known as the City Bowl, as it is in a basin and the heart of the city. It includes Foreshore, CBD, Bo-Kaap, Gardens, Higgovale, Tamboerskloof, Oranjezicht, Vredehoek, and Devil's Peak.

3. **Peninsula** is where Chapman's Peak Drive is found, as well as Hout Bay, Chapman's Peak Drive, Noordhoek, Kommetjie, Scarborough, Cape Point, Simon's Town, Fish Hoek, Kalk Bay, St James, and Muizenburg.

4. **Southern Suburbs** start at the base of Table Mountain and extend all the way to Cape Point.

This area includes Woodstock, Salt River, Observatory, Mowbray, Rosebank, Rondebosch, Newlands, Claremont, Kenilworth, Wynberg, Bishopscourt, Constantia, and Tokai.

5. **Cape Flats** is a main residential area made up of Athlone, Crossroads, Grassy Park, Gugulethu, Khayelitsha, Langa, Lansdowne, Manenberg, Mitchell's Plain, Nyanga, and Philippi.

6. **Blaauwberg Coast** is in the Western Cape and probably the fastest-growing area. It includes Paarden Island, Milnerton, Woodbridge Island, Sunset Beach, West Beach, Table View, Bloubergstrand, and Melkbosstrand.

7. **Northern Suburbs** is another residential area. It is comprised of Century City, Goodwood, Parow, Bellville, Welgemoed, Plattekloof, Tyger Valley, Durbanville, and Bellville.

8. **Helderberg** is a beautiful area full of coastline, vineyards, and the Helderberg Mountains. It

consists of Gordon's Bay, Somerset West, Strand, Sir Lowry's Pass, Macassar, and Lwandle.

The Port of Cape Town is deemed to be one of the busiest shipping corridors in the world. For that reason, one of its nicknames is "Tavern of the Seas." The Greenpoint Lighthouse is the oldest lighthouse in South Africa, dating back to 1824. It's also the headquarters for South Africa's Lighthouse Services. In 1929, an electric light that was visible twenty-five miles out to sea was installed in the lighthouse. Since thick winter fog is problematic, the beacon was outfitted with a booming foghorn that could be heard for miles. This earned the lighthouse the nickname "Moaning Minnie."

Most folks don't know there are penguins in Cape Town. Once known as Jackass Penguins, they are now called African Penguins. These cute critters can be found at Boulder's Beach.

**FYI: Cape Town was once called the
Cape of Storms but has long been dubbed a
much better name, "Mother City" of South
Africa. Remarkably, almost half of Cape
Town's population is under the age of 25!**

ANNUAL EVENTS & AVERAGE TEMPS

There are hundreds of festivals and special events held year round. Here is a list of some of the biggest and best. A comprehensive list can be found at www.capetown.travel.

Cape Minstrels Carnival (January) a spectacular New Year's celebration.
Up the Creek Music Festival (February) is three days of music, swimming, and partying.
Red Bull DHX (March) is an international race.
Cape Argus Pick 'n Pay Cycle Tour (March) is a fitness competition around the Cape Peninsula. Thousands of cyclists participate annually.
North Sea Jazz Festival (March) is a two-day jazz fest that is world renowned.
Old Mutual Two Oceans Marathon (April) is a 56km marathon with thousands competing.
SA Cheese Festival (April).
Taste of Cape Town (April).
MasterCard Cape Gourmet Food Festival (May) is a two-day food and wine festival

featuring top international chefs and food celebrities.

Cape Town Book Fair (June).

Currie Cup Rugby (July) is South America's biggest national rugby event.

Cape Town Fashion Week (August).

Hermanus Whale Festival (September).

Stellenbosch Food and Wine Festival (October) is a four-day celebration of fine wine and lots of entertainment options.

The Big Walk (October) is the biggest timed walk in the world.

Spier Festival (November) is held at the Spier Farm in Stellenbosch. There are lots of special events held in their amphitheater.

Kirstenbosch Sunday Summer Concerts (December) run from December to March with many different kinds of musical performances.

AVERAGE TEMPS

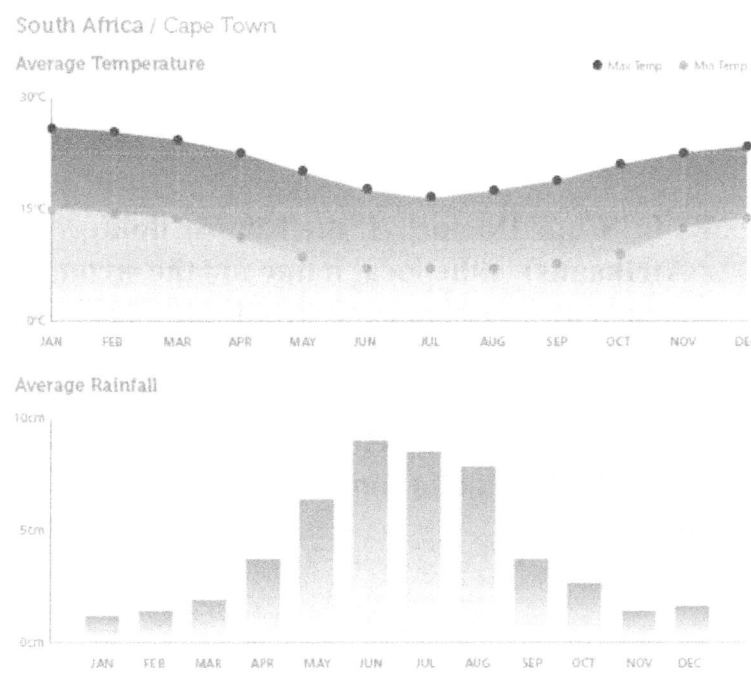

Cape Town has mild winters and summers.
Average summer temperatures (December –
February) are 60 - 80∘F (15 - 27∘C). During the
summer, there is sunshine for eleven hours a
day. In the winter (June – August) the temps
average 45 - 70∘F (7 - 20∘C). Rainfall is

moderate year round. Winds can be high year round (see FYI: Cape Doctor). The best time to visit is typically spring (September and October) and fall (April and May).

FYI: "Cape Doctor" ("die Kaapse dokter" in Afrikaans) is the local name for the strong, persistent, south-easterly wind that blows on the South African coast from spring to late summer It is known as the Cape Doctor because of a local belief that it clears Cape Town of pollution and 'pestilence'.

How to Pack

Cape Town is casual, so you should pack light:

*shorts

*sandals/flip flops/beach shoes

*walking shoes

*gear (scuba mask, etc.)

*bathing suit

*cotton blend shirts or blouses

*lightweight pants

*classic black dress (women) or sports jacket
(men) with matching shoes

*sunscreen and hat

*insect repellent

*raincoat or waterproof jacket

*waterproof bag (to safeguard phone, camera, etc.)

*toiletries and cosmetics

*medications

*documents

BONUS:
Excerpt from

Terrance Talks Travel:
A Pocket Guide to African Safaris

Terrance Zepke

Safari Publishing

CONTENTS

Introduction

I have been to Africa many times and still feel as if I've barely scratched the surface. There are so many things to do and see that it is a perfect vacation destination for all ages. In fact, one of the best family vacations you can have is a safari trip. Young and old can appreciate the many splendors and activities, such as a sunset cruise on the Zambezi River and seeing giraffes and gazelles up close during a bush walk. Africa holds a special place in my heart, and I am sure that it will for you too—if you decide to participate in this truly once-in-a-lifetime experience.

But there's a lot you need to know before you go. For one thing, Africa is a continent—not a country. Fifty-four countries make up this enormous continent. In fact, Africa is the second largest continent in the world. Africa makes up more than twenty percent of our world's land mass. It is three times bigger than the United States of America. Africa has more than 1 billion inhabitants from 3,000 ethnic groups. Each country has its own currency. Roughly 2,000 languages are spoken in Africa. South Africa alone has eleven official languages!

Some places in Africa are high in crime, just like other places around the world. Most of these are not even places where tourists go, such as The Democratic Republic of the Congo, Sudan, Somalia, and a few pockets of Nairobi and Zimbabwe. For the most part, however, Africa is quite safe.

While there are lots of other things to do in Africa besides safaris, let's face it, they are the main attraction—and rightfully so! For the most part, Africa's wildlife is confined to national parks and reserves. But then again, most of Africa is comprised of game reserves, World Heritage Sites, and national parks. There are hundreds, perhaps thousands, such places scattered throughout Africa. This book is about making sure travelers find the perfect safari experience *for them.* After all, a safari is not "one size fits all." One traveler may be looking for a particular experience, such as a birding safari in the Okavango Delta while another traveler is interested in gorilla trekking in Uganda. Some travelers will choose participatory camping safaris in Namibia while others prefer to stay in the luxurious William Holden Safari Club in East Africa. The point of this book is to make sure you know all the options and then take you step by step through the process of planning and booking your safari.

Subscribers to *Terrance Talks Travel* receive free travel reports, cheap travel tips, TRIP PICK OF THE WEEK, and are the first to learn about new episodes of ÜBER ADVENTURES. You'll also learn about book giveaways and contests, as well as receive a special sign up bonus. Visit www.terrancetalkstravel.com to subscribe to my blog and find archive episodes of

ÜBER ADVENTURES, including a few on Africa.

Safaris are among my favorite adventures, but since they are in sub-Saharan nations, travelers need to be prepared. After reading this reference, you'll learn everything you need to know. So keep reading and get ready for an adventure of a lifetime…

* * *

Chapter One

Step #1: Decide Where & How to Go

Africa is a continent with fifty-four countries. Where you go depends on what you want to see and do—and what your budget is. You can choose from $100 a day overland safaris that involve camping to $1,000 a day ultra-luxurious private safari lodges with suites and spas. But don't worry. There are lots of options in between these two extremes. But first, you need to figure out what you want to see and do.

FYI: The "Big Five" refers to Leopards, Lions, Rhinos, Elephants, and Cape Buffaloes. The "Big Nine" also includes Hippos, Cheetahs, Giraffes, and Zebras.

For most participants, the best safari experience
will be in Southern Africa or East Africa. In terms
of wildlife, both places offer roughly the same.
There are larger numbers of some animals in East
Africa's Masai Mara National Reserve and
Serengeti National Park, such as zebras and
wildebeests, while Southern Africa offers huge
numbers of lions and elephants.

However, in terms of topography, they are very
different. East Africa has miles of savannahs
while Southern Africa has the Skeleton Coast
(driest place in Africa), the Cape Peninsula
(whale watching and shark cage diving), and the
Okavango Delta (wetlands). East Africa has the
famed Mount Kilimanjaro while Southern Africa
offers Victoria Falls.

Another distinction is that participants enjoy
game drives in pop-up jeeps in East Africa,
meaning the roof pops up so that passengers can
stand up and take photos. In Southern Africa,
open air jeeps are used, meaning there is no roof!
Having experienced both, I would say that both
have their advantages and disadvantages. The

open air jeep gives you a more interactive experience, a real feel of being in the bush. However, when it is really hot or cold or rainy, I'll take the jeep with a roof—and A/C and heat. Also, foot safaris are not permitted in East Africa but can be achieved in many places in southern Africa.

Most first-time safari participants go to East Africa to the well-known Masai Mara and Serengeti, as well as Ngorongoro, Samburu, Amboseli, and Tsavo National Parks. They will be rewarded with lots of wildlife sightings and spectacular scenery.

While you can't go wrong on an East Africa safari, I think it is a more intimate experience in Southern Africa where there are more private game reserves. This means fewer tourists in any one place. The only place this is not true is in Kruger National Park, which always has lots of tourists. Private game reserves are owned or leased by private operators and range from moderate to luxurious in both amenities and pricing. There are also many other options to round out the safari experience, such as Cape Town including the Cape Peninsula and Cape Point, Johannesburg, Robben Island, Limpopo, Durban, and the Cape Winelands.

There may not be much of a decision as to where to go. Your safari destination may be determined by what you want to see. For example, the Black Rhino can only be found in Etosha National Park (Namibia), Kruger National Park (South Africa), and Chobe National Park (Botswana). The highest concentration of elephants is in South Africa's Addo National Park and Chobe National Park (Botswana). If you want to see the rare white lion, the only place is in South Africa's Timbavati region. If you're looking for a birding safari, they are all over Africa, especially in Kenya's Kakamega Forest and Botswana's Okavango Delta. If you want to see Victoria Falls, you have to go to Zambia and Zimbabwe. If you want a gorilla safari, you will go to Uganda or Rwanda, specifically Bwindi Impenetrable National Forest or Volcanoes National Park. If you want to go off the beaten path and are looking for the best bargain, that will be Malawi. If you're looking for maximum adventure activities, that would be South Africa, which offers unique options, such as kloofing, canopy tours, and shark cage diving.

You may notice 'Masai' is spelled two different ways: Maasai or Masai. Both ways are acceptable.

* * *

Best Safari Destinations…

As mentioned, the best safari destinations are East Africa and Southern Africa. Here's a list of the best destinations for each place:

Southern Africa=South Africa, Botswana, Namibia, Zimbabwe, Malawi, and Zambia.

East Africa=Kenya, Tanzania, Uganda, and Rwanda.

Highlights of each place:

Botswana: As far as tourism is concerned, this country is divided into five regions (Northern, Central, Kgalagadi, Eastern, and Southern). Safari participants will mostly be interested in the Northern and Central regions.

Northern Botswana: Okavango Delta (comprised of Panhandle, Delta, and Dryland), Moremi Game Reserve, and Chobe National Park.

Central Botswana: Central Kalahari Game Reserve (one of largest in the world), Kgalagadi Transfrontier Park (black-maned lion and 170 bird species), Makgadikgadi Pans National Park, and The Kgalagadi.

Best Park in Botswana: Chobe National Park is the third largest park in the country. It is the most biologically diverse with large numbers of birds, reptiles, and mammals, including the Kalahari Elephant. This is the largest in size of all known elephant species. A wide array of safaris are offered including boat safaris, canoe safaris, and game drives (classic safaris) where the Big Five (huge elephant population but low rhino population) can be seen.

http://www.botswanatourism.co.bw/

Kenya (East Africa): For the sake of tourism, it can be divided into Coastal Kenya, Northern

Kenya, Highlands & Valleys, Forests, and Wilderness Areas.

Highlands & Valleys: Mt. Kenya, Western Highlands, Rift Valley, and Menegai Crater.

Forests: Mt. Kenya Forest, Aberdare Forest, Kakamega Forest, and Arabuko Sokoke Forest.

Wilderness Areas: Masai Mara Game Reserve (home to Masai Mara tribe), Nairobi National Park, Samburu Game Reserve, Lake Nakuru National Park (home to thousands of flamingos), Amboseli National Park (specular views of Mt. Kilimanjaro), Buffalo Springs & Shaba National Reserve, Hell's Gate National Park, and Meru National Park.

Coastal Kenya: Tsavo East National Park and Tsavo West National Park. These two parks total roughly 8,000 miles.

Best Park in Kenya: Masai Mara National Reserve offers classic safaris where the Big Five (especially big cats) can be seen and where the annual wildebeest migration, which is the largest animal migration in the world, can be witnessed.

The largest population of lions can be found in
this reserve.

http://www.magicalkenya.com/

Wildebeest & Zebra Annual Migration

This event is the largest animal migration in the
world. We're talking about approximately 1.5
million (1.3 million wildebeest and 200,000+
zebras) migrating roughly 1,800 miles.

Where to go to see them?
The Serengeti and Masai Mara.

When?

This depends on a myriad of factors, but some believe the best time is Jan – March.

What else should I know?
They are unpredictable! They can be seen other times and places. The animals go forward, sideways, and backward (not in a straight line or circle, as popularly believed).

Malawi ("Warm Heart of Africa"): Lake Malawi National Park (is a UNESCO World Heritage Site and includes Mumbo Island), Liwonde National Park, Chongoni Rock Art Area (UNESCO World Heritage Site), Shire River (boat safari), Nyika National Park (wild and remote), Elephant Marsh, Majete Wildlife Reserve, Mount Mulanje, Monkey Bay, Kasungu National Park, Lengwe National Park. Malawi is separated from Mozambique and Tanzania by Lake Malawi. To its northwest is Zambia, to the northeast is Tanzania, and Mozambique is to its east, west, and south. There are several small game reserves here that have leopards, lions, hippos, and elephants, as well as lots of birds and antelopes.

Best Park in Malawi: Lake Malawi National Park has all kinds of wildlife, including vervet monkeys, warthogs, elephants, hippos, crocodiles, baboons, and hyrax. There are lots of beautiful tropical fish in Lake Malawi, as well as island camps. In addition to safaris, visitors can enjoy rock climbing, trekking, fishing, snorkeling, kayaking, and more.
http://www.malawitourism.com/

Namibia: Etosha National Park (one of the biggest and best parks in Africa), Skeleton Coast National Park (seal colonies, shipwrecks, huge dunes and canyons), Namib Naukluft National Park (nearly 20,000 square miles of lagoons, granite mountains, and savannahs), Mamili National Park, Damaraland, Fish River Canyon, Waterberg National Park, and Ai-Ais/Richtersveld Transfrontier Park.
Namibia is an adventure lover's paradise. Sky diving, rock climbing, quad biking, sandboarding, and more can be accomplished here.

Best Park in Namibia: Etosha National Park offers classic safaris with the Big Five (and flamingos seasonally). The park is home to several rare animals, such as black rhinos, Gemsbok, Tsessebe, and Black-faced Impalas. http://www.namibiatourism.org/

Namibia Safari

Rwanda: Volcanoes National Park (50 miles of lush vegetation and home to the endangered mountain gorilla and golden monkeys). It is the most patrolled park in the world and the oldest park in Africa. Other significant places: Akagera National Park, Gishwati Forest, and Nyungwe Forest National Park (East Africa's only canopy walk is offered here).

An East Africa Community Visa is now offered for those interested in traveling to Kenya, Uganda, and Rwanda. It is good for ninety days. More about this special travel visa can be found on the tourism site listed below.

Best Park in Rwanda: Volcanoes National Park is home to the mountain gorilla, as well as the golden monkey, buffalo, and spotted hyena, as well as 200 species of birds.

http://www.rwandatourism.com/

FYI: Rwanda and Uganda are where you go for gorilla safaris. You need to be in good physical shape to participate as you can trek in difficult terrain for 2 – 6 hours in search of the gorillas. If you don't avoid the rainy season, this will most likely be a wet trek.

South Africa: There are almost too many options for safaris in South Africa. Seriously! So I have narrowed it down to these top destinations: Golden Gate Highlands National Park, Karoo National Park, Kgalagadi Transfrontier Park, Knysna National Lake Area, Mapungubwe National Park, Marakele National Park, Mokala National Park, Kruger National Park, Namaqua National Park, Table Mountain National Park, Wilderness National Park, and Ai-Ais/Richtersveld Transfrontier Park.

Also worth mentioning are Grootbos Nature Reserve (100+ bird species and 500+ plant species), Sabi Sands (many private game reserves with lots of good wildlife viewing), and Kwazulu Natal (lots of small game reserves).

Best Park in South Africa: Kruger National Park is one of the biggest parks in all of Africa with more species of animals than anywhere else: 114 types of reptiles, 147 species of mammals, and 507 species of birds (and 336 types of trees). Classic safaris are offered here where all the Big Five can be seen, as well as many other species of animals.

Note: There is Kruger National Park and Greater Kruger National Park. Greater Kruger includes all the private reserves at Kruger. Greater Kruger is where walking safaris can be achieved

http://www.southafrica.net/za/en/landing/visitor-home

Tanzania (East Africa): There are many places in Tanzania so I have narrowed the list down to the top destinations: Ngorongoro Crater Park(includes Ngorongoro Crater, which is the largest intact caldera in world), Serengeti National Park, Zanzibar ("Spice Islands" and Zanzibar Archipelago), Tarangire National Park (third largest park in Tanzania), Lake Manyara

National Park, Mt. Kilimanjaro ("Roof of Africa"), Selous Game Reserve (second largest reserve in Tanzania and UNESCO World Heritage Site and great place for foot, boat, and classic safaris), Ruaha National Park, Mafia Island Marine Park, Serengeti National Park, Arusha National Park (forest animals), and Mt. Meru.

Best Park in Tanzania: Ngorongoro Crater Conservation Area is a UNESCO World Heritage Site. Its volcanic crater is one of the seven natural wonders of Africa. Walking safaris are permitted here and offer some of the best scenery and wildlife in Tanzania.
http://www.tanzaniatouristboard.com/

Uganda ("Pearl of Africa"): Bwindi Impenetrable Forest National Park (home to roughly 300 gorillas), Kibale National Park (rainforest, crater lakes, and grasslands), Kidepo Valley National Park, Lake Mburo National Park, Mgahinga National Park, Mount Elgon National Park, Semuliki National Park, Rwenzori National

Park, Murchison Falls National Park, and Queen
Elizabeth National Park (volcanic crater, lakes,
swamps, and rivers).

Best Park in Uganda: Kidepo Valley National
Park accommodates many species found nowhere
else in Uganda, such as the cheetah, black-backed
jackals, Burchell's Zebra, Bush Duiker,
waterbuck, side-striped jackals, Cape Buffalo,
and Rothschild's Giraffe. It boasts close to 500
species of birds, including many birds of prey,
such as Egyptian Vulture and Pygmy Falcon.
http://visituganda.com/

Zambia: South Luangwa National Park, North Luangwa National Park (both have good variety of lesser seen wildlife, such as hyenas, pukus, and elands), Liuwa Plain National Park, Lochinvar National Park, Luambe National Park, Lukusuzi National Park, Kafue National Park (one of the largest in Africa), Blue Lagoon National Park, Isangano National Park, Lusenga Plain National Park, Mosi-oa-Tunva National Park, Mweru Wantipa National Park, Kasanka National Park, Lavushi Manda National Park, Nsumbu National Park, Nyika National Park, West Lunga National Park, Sioma Ngwezi National Park, and the Lower Zambezi National Park (offers many safari options, such as boat, canoe, walking, and night safaris), including Victoria Falls.

Anything you can imagine (and then some!) can be done while at Victoria Falls, such as swimming in Devils Pool (seasonally), rafting, helicopter rides, micro lighting ("Flight of Angels"), hydrospeeding, bungee jumping, gorge swinging, and abseiling. It is truly an adventure lover's paradise.

Best Park in Zambia: South Luangwa National Park has large populations of elephants, Thornicroft Giraffes, hippos, crocodiles, and buffalos. It is one of the best parks in Africa for walking safaris and one of only a few places where night walking safaris are offered. http://www.zambiatourism.com/

Zimbabwe: Hwange National Park (biggest park in Zimbabwe and home to diverse animal population including rhinos, elephants, and giraffes), Chizarira National Park (wild and remote), Zambezi National Park, Mt. Inyangani (highest mountain in Zimbabwe), Chimanimani National Park, Kazuma Pan National Park, Matopos National Park, Nyanga National Park, Gonarezhou National Park (wild and remote), Zambezi River (and Victoria Falls, which is twice the height of Niagara Falls and nearly twice the width is in Victoria Falls National Park), Mana Pools National Park (in Zambezi Valley), Matobo Hills National Park, Matusadona National Park, and Malilangwe Wildlife Reserve (best place to see rare species, such as sable antelope).

Just like in Zambia, there are the roughly the same amount of adventure activities offered. Also, while there you may want to check out Great Zimbabwe, an ancient city, and UNESCO World Heritage Site.

Best Park in Zimbabwe: Hwange National Park is home to the Big Five, as well as many other animals not commonly seen in other places in Africa, such as the Black-faced hunting dog, leopard, white and black rhinos, and cheetahs, as well as 50 species of raptors, that can be seen during classic safaris. This park is the size of the country of Wales. It is the oldest and largest in the country. It was named after a local Nhanzwa Chief, Hwange Roseumbani.

http://www.zimbabwetourism.net/

How about adding an island stay onto your safari?

Lots of folks choose to finish their safari with a short stay on one of Africa's lovely islands. In addition to resort activities, there are national parks, reserves, and abundant wildlife on these islands. Here is a list of the best African islands:

Madagascar: This is the fourth largest island in the world with a unique ecosystem and hundreds of rare or endangered wildlife (including 103 lemur species, forest elephants, giant forest hogs, two dozen species of bats, 200 species of butterflies, and 300+ species of birds) and unique flora and fauna. National Parks include Amber Mountain, Andohahela, Zombitse-Vohibasia, Zahamena, Tsimanampetsotse, Bemaraha, Isalo, Perinet Reserve, Mantadia, Marojeijy, Ranomafana, Namoroka, Midongy du Sud, Masoala, Andringitra, Ankarafantsika, Baie de Baly, and Kirindy Mitea. http://www.world-guides.com/africa/madagascar/

Mauritius: This is a bustling, luxurious island full of five-star resort hotels, specialty restaurants, and beautiful beaches. National Parks include Black River Gorges, Islets, and Bras d'Eau. http://www.mauritius.net/index.php

Mozambique: It is known for snorkeling, great scuba diving, whale watching, birding, and world-class game fishing, as well as the Bazaruto Archipelago (Bazaruto, Benguerra, and Margaruque Islands). National Parks include Gorongosa, Niassa, Banhine, Bazaruto, Limpopo, Magoe, Zinave, and Quirimbas. http://www.visitmozambique.net/

Republic of Seychelles: This is a compilation of 115 islands in the western Indian Ocean. Tourists flock to Felicite, Fregate, Cousine, Denis, Bird, Desroches, Mahe, Praslin, and La Digue. While it has become a popular destination with the rich and famous, the Seychelles has a wide range of affordable hotels, self-caterings, and charming Creole guesthouses. National Parks include Baie Ternay, Curieuse, Ile Coco, Morne Seychelles,

Port Launay, Praslin, Silhouette, and Ste. Anne.
http://www.seychelles.travel/

Zanzibar: This Indian Ocean Island is only twenty or so miles from Tanzania. Some claim it has the best fishing, diving, and snorkeling in the world. Stone Town is historic and picturesque. There are a few small reserves, including Zala, Kiwengwa, and Ngezi, as well as seven marine parks. The only national park on the island is the Jozani Chwaka Bay National Park. This 20-mile park is home to many species of birds and monkeys, as well as flora and fauna. http://www.zanzibartourism.net/

**Mountain gorillas
(Uganda & Rwanda)**

A **UNESCO World Heritage Site** is a place (such as a forest, mountain, lake, island, desert, monument, building, complex, or city) that is listed by the United Nations Educational, Scientific and Cultural Organization (UNESCO) as of special cultural or physical significance (see list of World Heritage Sites). There are quite a few such places in Africa, including Okavango Delta, Victoria Falls, Ngorongoro Conservation Area, Bwindi Impenetrable Forest, Tsingy Reserve, Mana Pools, and Mt. Kilimanjaro.

For a complete list:
http://en.wikipedia.org/wiki/List_of_World_Heri tage_Sites_in_Africaa

Here is a list of different types of safaris. For certain safaris, you will not have a choice. For example, foot safaris are what you'll do in Madagascar. You will trek if you choose a gorilla safari. You will participate in a classic safari (game drives) in Kenya.

Driving safaris (also known as overland safaris): typically participants book a safari package, and upon arrival, they are met by their guide and driver, who takes them from reserve to reserve (or park) where they will see wildlife during **classic game drives**. These overland safari packages are offered by tour operators specializing in travel to Africa. This is the most popular safari option. There is a list of tour operators in the back of this reference.

NOTE: Additional activities that can be booked through a tour operator or through the lodge or on your own include a hot-air balloon flight, elephant encounter or ride, fishing at Lake Victoria, Victoria Falls cruise, visits to local schools or villages, shark cage diving, and much

more (depending on destination) can be added on
to these packages. See below for more on these
options.

Bush walks are permitted in certain places in
addition to classic game drives or in lieu of them.
For example, most places in East Africa do not
allow them, but South Africa does. However,
South Africa's biggest safari destination, Kruger
National Park, does not permit bush walks, but
most private game reserves at Kruger permit
them.

Specialty Safaris are another option. Travelers
can create a customized safari or work with a
travel agent to create a special safari just for them.
This can be a private safari or one that is simply
independent, meaning you may be in a small
group sometimes but you are not traveling with
the same group throughout as you do on an
overland safari. Even if you plan to book a safari
package, you should be aware of all the options
so that you can put together the best possible trip.
For most travelers, this is a once in a lifetime trip,

so you want to be sure you know about every
opportunity, such as an extension to Victoria Falls
or a short stay at an African island resort at the
end of your safari. Some folks think this option is
more expensive, but I have put together
customized safaris that cost less than most safari
packages.

Self-drive safaris are for those who are
comfortable traveling independently and who feel
they can handle whatever might happen. In other
words, you are truly on your own. You plan your
trip, book the trip, rent a car, and drive yourself
wherever you plan to go. I don't recommend this
option for most folks for several reasons. For one
thing, this is not the same as traveling on your
own in Europe or the U.S. These are developing
countries with a completely different tourism
infrastructure. Some of these areas are not safe for
tourists or have poor roads that can be difficult to
navigate. However, if you are determined this is
what you want to do, be meticulous in your
planning. Stick to main roads and parks. That

said, most parks are in remote places, so there is always a chance you will get lost or run out of gas or get a flat tire.

Make sure you are ready in case of an emergency. Be sure to have at least one spare tire, extra fuel, food, water, and a first-aid kit. Be sure you have left your itinerary with a trusted friend or family member before you depart so that if anything happens, they will have some idea of where you are.

For those with limited time and unlimited funds, **fly-in safaris** are an option. There are charter flights that take participants right to the game reserve or park. This is also a good option for visiting places that are practically inaccessible even in an all-terrain vehicle. It's also good for maximizing your time as flying is always faster than driving. These are usually offered in Namibia, Botswana, Zambia, and Zimbabwe.

Walking safaris are different from bush walks. Bush walks (South Africa, Botswana, and Namibia) are the equivalent of a game drive, which lasts 2-3 hours. Foot safaris are extended game drives whereby you might be walking through a portion of a game reserve for most of a day. In other words, your safari experience is on foot rather than in a jeep or a boat. You are walking in the wilds of Africa! You are having an authentic safari experience, like safari participants used to have once upon a time. These special safaris are only offered in Zimbabwe and Zambia.

A few places permit elephant-back safaris. Instead of achieving your safari on foot or through the game drive, you do it on an elephant. **The best place for an elephant-back safari is the Okavango Delta in Botswana.**

Another option is a **canoe safari**. The best places for canoe safaris are on the Okavango River in the Okavango Delta and the Zambezi River (Zambia and Zimbabwe). Participants leisurely float down the river in mokoros with guides pointing out wildlife.

Botswana Canoe Safari

Boat safaris are offered in Malawi, Zimbabwe, Botswana, and Zambia. More about boat and cruise safaris can be found in the back of this reference.

Hot-air balloon safaris are offered many places throughout Africa, but I think the best is East Africa over the Northern Serengeti. You will watch the sun rise over the Serengeti and see so much wildlife—it is just a thrilling experience! Some places in South Africa offer them but make sure they are wildlife safaris as some of those are scenic rides over the Cape Winelands and townships. Typically, the rides last 2-3 hours and take place in the early morning. Note that you may have to miss a game drive to participate in the balloon safari, but it is worth it! Often, a champagne breakfast is served in the bush.

Camel safaris are another option participants can choose in Namibia, Kenya, and Tanzania. They

are typically led by local tribesman and riding a
camel is a memorable experience!

Or you can opt to take a **horseback safari or a
biking safari,** but this is only a good option for
experienced riders.

For the less adventurous, there are cruise lines
that offer good African itineraries, as well as
safari cruises on the Zambezi River or Nile
River.

About Lodging…

Accommodations in Africa are as diverse as the topography and people. One option is a **mobile tent safari.** As the name suggests, the camp is mobile. Upon arrival at the next destination, you will find the staff has already arrived and set up camp. But there is no "roughing it" as you will have hot showers, good food, lovely tents, and bar service. Another option is **participatory camping** whereby you help set up and break down camp, as well as help prepare meals. This is a great option for budget-minded and adventurous travelers. There are not as many amenities, but the trade-off is the authentic safari experience. You are camping in the bush!

Another option is that your small group will move from location to location but will stay in **lodges,** such as Kampala Lodge in South Africa or you may stay in **permanent tented camps,** such as Gorilla Sanctuary Camp in Uganda. You are accompanied by a knowledgeable guide and driver. These lodges and camps range from two-

star to five-star, and the price is in accordance
with its rating.

*Excerpted from **TERRANCE TALKS TRAVEL: A
Pocket Guide to African Safaris**©*

Dear Reader,

Thank you for your interest in *TERRANCE TALKS TRAVEL: The Quirky Tourist Guide to Cape Town.* I spent a great deal of time compiling this information into what I believe is an easy-to-read, useful reference. I would love to hear from you if you'd like to post a question or comment about this book or anything travel-related on www.terrancetalkstravel.com. I do respond to all comments. If you'd like to get lots of travel tips be sure to sign up for my *Terrance Talks Travel* blog, which will also alert you when the latest episodes of my travel show are available and reveal my weekly TRIP PICK.

I would also like to ask you to please share your feedback about this book on Amazon or your favorite bookseller so that other readers might discover this title too.

Authors appreciate readers more than you realize and we dearly love and depend upon good reviews! If you've never posted a review before it is easy to do…just tell folks what you liked or didn't like about this book and why you (hopefully) recommend it. http://www.amazon.com/Terrance-Zepke/e/B000APJNIA/ref=sr_ntt_srch_lnk_3?qid=1438800300&sr=8-3.

Happy travels!

Terrance

TERRANCE ZEPKE
Series Reading Order
& Guide

Series List

Most Haunted Series
Terrance Talks Travel Series
Cheap Travel Series
Spookiest Series
Stop Talking Series
Carolinas for Kids Series
Ghosts of the Carolinas Series
Books & Guides for the Carolinas Series
& More Books by Terrance Zepke

≈

Introduction

Here is a list of titles by Terrance Zepke. They are presented in chronological order although they do not need to be read in any particular order.

Also included is an author bio, a personal message from Terrance, and some other information you may find helpful.

All books are available as eBooks and print books. They can be found on all major booksellers or through your favorite independent bookseller.

For more about this author and her books visit her Author Page at:
http://www.amazon.com/Terrance-Zepke/e/B000APJNIA/.

You can also connect with Terrance on Twitter @terrancezepke or on

www.facebook.com/terrancezepke
www.pinterest.com/terrancezepke
www.goodreads.com/terrancezepke

Sign up for weekly email notifications of the *Terrance Talks Travel* blog and receive a FREE 50-page CHEAP TRAVEL REPORT and be the first to learn about new episodes of Uber Adventures, cheap travel tips & resources, and her TRIP PICK OF THE WEEK at www.terrancetalkstravel.com or sign up for her *Mostly Ghostly* blog at www.terrancezepke.com.

You can follow her travel show, **TERRANCE
TALKS TRAVEL: ÜBER ADVENTURES on**
www.blogtalkradio.com/terrancetalkstravel
or subscribe to it on **iTunes.**

*Warning: Listening to this show could
lead to a spectacular South African
safari, hot-air ballooning over the Swiss
Alps, Disney Adventures, and Tornado
Tours!*

Terrance Zepke is co-host of the writing show,
**A WRITER'S JOURNEY: FROM BLANK
PAGE TO PUBLISHED.** All episodes can be
found on **iTunes** or www.terrancezepke.com.

≈

AUTHOR BIO

Terrance Zepke studied Journalism at the
University of Tennessee and later received a
Master's degree in Mass Communications from
the University of South Carolina. She studied
parapsychology at the renowned Rhine Research
Center.

Zepke spends much of her time happily traveling
around the world but always returns home to the
Carolinas where she lives part-time in both states.
She has written hundreds of articles and close to
three dozen books. She is the host of *Terrance
Talks Travel: Über Adventures* and co-host of *A
Writer's Journey: From Blank Page to Published.*
Additionally, this award-winning and best-selling
author has been featured in many publications
and programs, such as NPR, CNN, The
Washington Post, Associated Press, Travel with
Rick Steves, Around the World, Publishers
Weekly, World Travel & Dining with Pierre
Wolfe, Good Morning Show, The Learning
Channel, and The Travel Channel.

When she's not investigating haunted places,
searching for pirate treasure, or climbing
lighthouses, she is most likely packing for her

next adventure to some far flung place, such as Reykjavik or Kwazulu Natal. Some of her favorite adventures include piranha fishing on the Amazon, shark cage diving in South Africa, hiking the Andes Mountains Inca Trail, camping in the Himalayas, dog-sledding in the Arctic Circle, and a gorilla safari in the Congo.

≈

MOST HAUNTED SERIES

A Ghost Hunter's Guide to the Most Haunted Places in America (2012)
https://read.amazon.com/kp/embed?asin=B0085SG22O
&preview=newtab&linkCode=kpe&ref_=cm_sw_r_kb_
dp_zerQwb1AMJ0R4

A Ghost Hunter's Guide to the Most Haunted Houses in America (2013)
https://read.amazon.com/kp/embed?asin=B00C3PUMG
C&preview=newtab&linkCode=kpe&ref_=cm_sw_r_kb
_dp_BfrQwb1WF1Y6T

A Ghost Hunter's Guide to the Most Haunted Hotels & Inns in America (2014)
https://read.amazon.com/kp/embed?asin=B00C3PUMG
C&preview=newtab&linkCode=kpe

A Ghost Hunter's Guide to the Most Haunted Historic Sites in America (2016)
https://www.amazon.com/Ghost-Hunters-Haunted-
Historic-America-
ebook/dp/B01LXADK90/ref=sr_1_1?s=books&ie=UTF
8&qid=1475973918&sr=1-
1&keywords=a+ghost+hunter%27s+guide+to+the+most
+haunted+historic+sites+in+america

*The Ghost Hunter's MOST HAUNTED Box Set (3 in 1):
Discover America's Most Haunted Destinations* (2016)
https://read.amazon.com/kp/embed?asin=B01HISAAJM
&preview=newtab&linkCode=kpe&ref_=cm_sw_r_kb_
dp_ulz-xbNKND7VT

*A Ghost Hunter's Guide to the Most Haunted Places in
the World* (2018)
https://read.amazon.com/kp/embed?asin=B078ZL382D
&preview=newtab&linkCode=kpe&ref_=cm_sw_r_kb_
dp_nVNXAb61HF42W

≈

TERRANCE TALKS TRAVEL SERIES

Terrance Talks Travel: A Pocket Guide to South Africa (2015)
https://read.amazon.com/kp/embed?asin=B00PSTFTLI&
preview=newtab&linkCode=kpe&ref_=cm_sw_r_kb_dp
_pirQwb12XZX65

Terrance Talks Travel: A Pocket Guide to African Safaris (2015)
https://read.amazon.com/kp/embed?asin=B00PSTFZSA
&preview=newtab&linkCode=kpe&ref_=cm_sw_r_kb_
dp_jhrQwb0P8Z87G

Terrance Talks Travel: A Pocket Guide to Adventure Travel (2015)
https://read.amazon.com/kp/embed?asin=B00UKMAVQ
G&preview=newtab&linkCode=kpe&ref_=cm_sw_r_kb
_dp_ThrQwb1PVVZAZ

Terrance Talks Travel: A Pocket Guide to Florida Keys (including Key West & The Everglades) (2016)
https://read.amazon.com/kp/embed?asin=B01EWHML5
8&preview=newtab&linkCode=kpe&ref_=cm_sw_r_kb
_dp_YMbHybP0ZZEFK

Terrance Talks Travel: The Quirky Tourist Guide to Key West (2017) https://www.amazon.com/Terrance-Zepke/e/B000APJNIA/ref=sr_ntt_srch_lnk_1?qid=1485052308&sr=8-1

Terrance Talks Travel: The Quirky Tourist Guide to Cape Town (2017) https://www.amazon.com/Terrance-Zepke/e/B000APJNIA/ref=sr_ntt_srch_lnk_1?qid=1485052308&sr=8-1

African Safari Box Set: Featuring TERRANCE TALKS TRAVEL: *A Pocket Guide to South Africa* and *TERRANCE TALKS TRAVEL: A Pocket Guide to African Safaris* (2017) https://read.amazon.com/kp/embed?asin=B01MUH6VJU&preview=newtab&linkCode=kpe&ref_=cm_sw_r_kb_dp_xLFLybAQKFA0B

Terrance Talks Travel: The Quirky Tourist Guide to Reykjavik (2017) https://www.amazon.com/Terrance-Zepke/e/B000APJNIA/ref=sr_ntt_srch_lnk_15?qid=1488514258&sr=8-15

Terrance Talks Travel: The Quirky Tourist Guide to Charleston, South Carolina (2017) https://www.amazon.com/Terrance-Zepke/e/B000APJNIA/ref=sr_ntt_srch_lnk_15?qid=1488514258&sr=8-15

Terrance Talks Travel: The Quirky Tourist Guide to Ushuaia (2017)
https://www.amazon.com/Terrance-Zepke/e/B000APJNIA/ref=sr_ntt_srch_lnk_15?qid=1488514258&sr=8-15

Terrance Talks Travel: The Quirky Tourist Guide to Antarctica (2017) https://www.amazon.com/Terrance-Zepke/e/B000APJNIA/ref=sr_ntt_srch_lnk_1?qid=1489092624&sr=8-1

TERRANCE TALKS TRAVEL: The Quirky Tourist Guide to Machu Picchu & Cuzco (Peru) 2017
https://read.amazon.com/kp/embed?asin=B07147HLQY&preview=newtab&linkCode=kpe&ref_=cm_sw_r_kb_dp_HmZmzb9FT5E0P

Terrance Talks Travel: A Pocket Guide to East Africa's Uganda and Rwanda (2018)
https://read.amazon.com/kp/embed?asin=B079YN892B&preview=newtab&linkCode=kpe&ref_=cm_sw_r_kb_dp_RWvQAbR3KQVQM

TERRANCE TALKS TRAVEL: The Quirky Tourist Guide to Kathmandu (Nepal) & The Himalayas (2018)
https://www.amazon.com/Terrance-Zepke/e/B000APJNIA/ref=dp_byline_cont_ebooks_1

≈

CHEAP TRAVEL SERIES

How to Cruise Cheap! (2017)

https://www.amazon.com/Cruise-Cheap-CHEAP-TRAVEL-Book-ebook/dp/B01N6NYM1N/

How to Fly Cheap! (2017)

https://www.amazon.com/How-Cheap-CHEAP-TRAVEL-Book-ebook/dp/B01N7Q81YG/

How to Travel Cheap! (2017)

https://www.amazon.com/Terrance-Zepke/e/B000APJNIA/

How to Travel FREE or Get Paid to Travel! (2017)

https://www.amazon.com/Terrance-Zepke/e/B000APJNIA/

CHEAP TRAVEL SERIES (4 IN 1) BOX SET (2017)
https://read.amazon.com/kp/embed?asin=B071ZGV1TY&preview=newtab&linkCode=kpe&ref_=cm_sw_r_kb_dp_.VNXAb8HMFQDY

≈

SPOOKIEST SERIES

Spookiest Lighthouses (2013)
https://read.amazon.com/kp/embed?asin=B00EAAQA2S
&preview

Spookiest Battlefields (2015)
https://read.amazon.com/kp/embed?asin=B00XUSWS3
G&preview=newtab&linkCode=kpe&ref_=cm_sw_r_kb
_dp_okrQwb0TR9F8M

Spookiest Cemeteries (2016)
http://www.amazon.com/Terrance-
Zepke/e/B000APJNIA/ref=sr_ntt_srch_lnk_1?qid=1457
641303&sr=8-1

*Spookiest Box Set (3 in 1): Discover America's Most
Haunted Destinations* (2016)
https://read.amazon.com/kp/embed?asin=B01HH2OM4I
&preview=newtab&linkCode=kpe&ref_=cm_sw_r_kb_
dp_Anz-xbT3SDEZS

Spookiest Objects (2017)
https://read.amazon.com/kp/embed?asin=B0728FMVZF
&preview=newtab&linkCode=kpe&ref_=cm_sw_r_kb_
dp_TXNXAbS0DF352

MOST HAUNTED and SPOOKIEST Sampler Box Set:
Featuring *A GHOST HUNTER'S GUIDE TO THE MOST
HAUNTED PLACES IN AMERICA* and *SPOOKIEST
CEMETERIES* (2017)

https://read.amazon.com/kp/embed?asin=B01N17EEOM
&preview=newtab&linkCode=kpe&ref_=cm_sw_r_kb_
dp_.JFLybCTN3QEF

≈

STOP TALKING SERIES

Stop Talking & Start Writing Your Book (2015)
https://read.amazon.com/kp/embed?asin=B012YHTIAY
&preview=newtab&linkCode=kpe&ref_=cm_sw_r_kb_
dp_qlrQwb1N7G3YF

Stop Talking & Start Publishing Your Book (2015)
https://read.amazon.com/kp/embed?asin=B013HHV1LE
&preview=newtab&linkCode=kpe&ref_=cm_sw_r_kb_
dp_WlrQwb1F63MFD

Stop Talking & Start Selling Your Book (2015)
https://read.amazon.com/kp/embed?asin=B015YAO33K
&preview=newtab&linkCode=kpe&ref_=cm_sw_r_kb_
dp_ZkrQwb188J8BE

*Stop Talking & Start Writing Your Book Series (3 in 1)
Box Set* (2016) https://www.amazon.com/Stop-Talking-
Start-Writing-Box-
ebook/dp/B01M58J5AZ/ref=sr_1_5?s=books&ie=UTF8
&qid=1475974073&sr=1-
5&keywords=stop+talking+and+start+writing

≈

CAROLINAS FOR KIDS SERIES

Lighthouses of the Carolinas for Kids (2009)
http://www.amazon.com/Lighthouses-Carolinas-Kids-Terrance-Zepke/dp/1561644293/ref=asap_bc?ie=UTF8

Pirates of the Carolinas for Kids (2009)
https://read.amazon.com/kp/embed?asin=B01BJ3VSWK&preview=newtab&linkCode=kpe&ref_=cm_sw_r_kb_dp_rGrXwb0XDTSTA

Ghosts of the Carolinas for Kids (2011)
https://read.amazon.com/kp/embed?asin=B01BJ3VSVQ&preview=newtab&linkCode=kpe&ref_=cm_sw_r_kb_dp_XLrXwb0E7N1AK

≈

GHOSTS OF THE CAROLINAS SERIES

Ghosts of the Carolina Coasts (1999)
http://www.amazon.com/Ghosts-Carolina-Coasts-Terrance-Zepke/dp/1561641758/ref=asap_bc?ie=UTF8

The Best Ghost Tales of South Carolina (2004)
http://www.amazon.com/Best-Ghost-Tales-South-Carolina/dp/1561643068/ref=asap_bc?ie=UTF8

Ghosts & Legends of the Carolina Coasts (2005)
https://read.amazon.com/kp/embed?asin=B01AGQJAB
W&preview=newtab&linkCode=kpe&ref_=cm_sw_r_k
b_dp_VKrXwb1Q09794

The Best Ghost Tales of North Carolina (2006)
https://read.amazon.com/kp/embed?asin=B01BJ3VSV6
&preview=newtab&linkCode=kpe&ref_=cm_sw_r_kb_
dp_6IrXwb0XKT90Q

≈

BOOKS & GUIDES FOR THE CAROLINAS SERIES

Pirates of the Carolinas (2005)
http://www.amazon.com/Pirates-Carolinas-Terrance-
Zepke/dp/1561643440/ref=asap_bc?ie=UTF8

Coastal South Carolina: Welcome to the Lowcountry
(2006)
http://www.amazon.com/Coastal-South-Carolina-
Welcome-
Lowcountry/dp/1561643483/ref=asap_bc?ie=UTF8

*Coastal North Carolina: Its Enchanting Islands, Towns
& Communities* (2011)
http://www.amazon.com/Coastal-North-Carolina-
Terrance-Zepke/dp/1561645117/ref=asap_bc?ie=UTF8

Lighthouses of the Carolinas: A Short History & Guide
(2011)
https://read.amazon.com/kp/embed?asin=B01AGQJA7G
&preview=newtab&linkCode=kpe&ref_=cm_sw_r_kb_
dp_UHrXwb09A22P1

≈

MORE BOOKS BY TERRANCE ZEPKE

Lowcountry Voodoo: Tales, Spells & Boo Hags (2009)
https://read.amazon.com/kp/embed?asin=B018WAGUC
6&preview=newtab&linkCode=kpe&ref_=cm_sw_r_kb
_dp_UmrQwb19AVSYG

*The Encyclopedia of Cheap Travel: Save Up to 90% on
Lodging, Flights, Tours, Cruises & More!* (2011)
https://read.amazon.com/kp/embed?asin=B005WKGNK
Y&preview=newtab&linkCode=kpe&ref_=cm_sw_r_kb
_dp_InrQwb18QTWGS

Ghosts of Savannah (2012)
http://www.amazon.com/Ghosts-Savannah-Terrance-
Zepke/dp/1561645303/ref=asap_bc?ie=UTF8

*How To Train Your Puppy or Dog Using Three Simple
Strategies* (FUN & FAST!) 2017
https://www.amazon.com/Train-Puppy-Using-Simple-
Strategies-ebook/dp/B01MZ5GN2M/

*Fiction books were written under a pseudonym

≈

INDEX

I

Iziko Slave Lodge, 36
Iziko South African Museum and Planetarium, 36
Iziko South African National Gallery, 36

J

Johannesburg, 8, 10, 11, 12, 76, 99

K

Kenya, 9, 25, 100, 102, 104, 105, 110, 123, 130
Kirstenbosch National Botanical Garden, 22, 37
Knysna Forest, 49
Kruger National Park, 98, 99, 111, 112, 124

L

Lion's Head, 77
Little Karoo, 50

M

Machu Picchu, 147
Malay Quarter. *See* Bo Kaap
Melktert
    recipe, 65
Mossel Bay, 47
Muizenberg, 53
Muizenburg, 78

N

Nairobi, 9

Made in the USA
Columbia, SC
06 December 2018